JAN '04

363.3481 Binney, Greg A.
BINNEY

Careers in the
Federal Emergency
Management Agency's
search and rescue
units.

$26.50

DATE			

CAREERS IN SEARCH AND RESCUE OPERATIONS

CAREERS IN THE

FEDERAL EMERGENCY MANAGEMENT AGENCY'S

SEARCH AND RESCUE UNITS

Greg A. Binney

the rosen publishing group's

rosen
central

Published in 2003 by The Rosen Publishing Group, Inc.
29 East 21st Street, New York, NY 10010

First Edition

Library of Congress Cataloging-in-Publication Data

Binney, Greg A.
Careers in the Federal Emergency Management Agency's search and rescue units / Greg A. Binney.— 1st ed.
    p. cm. — (Careers in search and rescue operations)
Includes bibliographical references and index.
ISBN 0-8239-3832-8 (lib. bdg.)
1. United States. Federal Emergency Management Agency—Vocational guidance. 2. Rescue work—United States. 3. Search and rescue operations—United States. 4. Emergency management—United States.
I. Title. II. Series.
HV551.3 B56 2003
363.34'81'02373—dc21

                                       2002013172

Manufactured in the United States of America

CONTENTS

INTRODUCTION

A Day at Ground Zero

September 11, 2001: The day of the horrifying terrorist attacks on New York City's World Trade Center and the Pentagon outside Washington, D.C. In the time it took for planes to crash into three of the most important buildings on the planet, thousands of people were killed or injured.

The September 11 terrorist attacks were the largest man-made disaster in the history of the United States. And although the consequences were unforgettably tragic, they would have been much worse if it hadn't been for the many brave men, women, and dogs who risked their lives to help rescue and recover victims of this disaster. Among the heroic rescuers were over 800 workers belonging to the Federal Emergency Management Agency's Urban Search and Rescue Task Forces.

The Federal Emergency Management Agency, or FEMA, is a national agency that organizes rescue teams specialized in dealing with all types of national disasters. Almost immediately after the attack on the World Trade Center, eight FEMA

Emergency workers and firefighters sift through the rubble of the collapsed World Trade Center in New York City on September 18, 2001, a week after the worst terrorist attack on American soil. Clean-up efforts continued for roughly nine months.

search and rescue task forces were on site at Ground Zero, helping to support the Fire Department of New York (FDNY) and other rescue agencies.

Eight days later, on September 19, these rescue workers were still working around the clock, searching for survivors amidst the nightmarish collapse of concrete, steel, crushed furniture, and dust. The work was physically and emotionally draining, not to mention extremely dangerous. Smoke and toxic gases made breathing difficult. Slabs of rubble could give way and collapse at any moment, causing serious injuries.

Emergency workers surrounded by smoke, grime, and deadly fumes at Ground Zero in New York City. Search and rescue workers often work in dangerous and unhealthy conditions.

Above all, there was the horror of sifting through piles of debris and finding victims.

Many members of FEMA task forces are professional firefighters who deal with disasters on a daily basis. However, others are specialists such as doctors, engineers, communications experts, and dog handlers who have trained for years to be on these teams and to be able to participate in these disaster operations. They aren't paid for the hours they spend in training—they do it because they truly believe they can make a difference. And they do.

When they weren't at Ground Zero, team members were shuttled across New York City to their temporary camp: an ocean of tents and cots spread across the concrete floor of Manhattan's gigantic Jacob Javitz Convention Center.

"After transport, briefing, and eating, we get maybe four or five hours to sleep," said Joe Brocato, a rescue specialist with FEMA's Pennsylvania Task Force, in an interview published on FEMA's Web site on September 19, 2001. "We work, work, work, then pull back and have to wait while they move huge girders and other heavy objects," Brocato said. "It's tedious. At times it's frustrating. But it is an honor to be here."

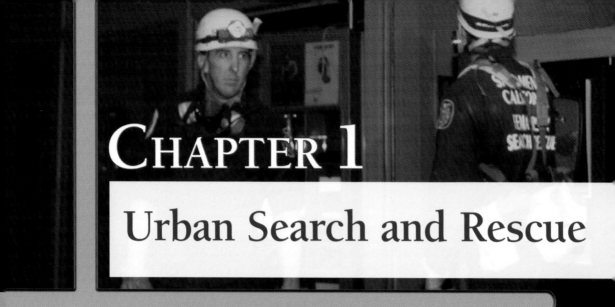

CHAPTER 1

Urban Search and Rescue

A disaster can strike at any time, in any place. Sometimes, it can develop over days or weeks—as is the case with hurricanes. Other times, a disaster can strike suddenly, right out of the blue, as with an earthquake or a terrorist attack.

Disasters can be natural such as earthquakes, hurricanes, tidal waves, volcanoes, floods, tornadoes, mudslides, avalanches, or fires. Human beings can also produce disasters: Oil spills, collapsed buildings, and the leakage of dangerous gases or radioactive materials such as plutonium are examples of disasters that are the result of human error. Terrorist acts, such as the 1995 bombing of the Alfred P. Murrah Federal Building in Oklahoma City and the terrorist attacks on the World Trade Center and the Pentagon on September 11, 2001, are also man-made disasters.

Each year, North Americans (like people all over the world), have to deal with disasters and their destructive and frightening consequences. When disaster strikes in the United States,

FEMA helps with all sorts of natural disasters. The above photo—released by FEMA—shows a collapsed home at Kitty Hawk, North Carolina, that was devastated by Hurricane Dennis in 1999.

FEMA (Federal Emergency Management Agency)

FEMA is an independent government agency that reports directly to the president of the United States. Its mission, as quoted on FEMA's Web site, is:

"To reduce loss of life and property and protect [America's] critical infrastructure from all types of hazards through a comprehensive, risk-based, emergency management program of mitigation [reducing danger], preparedness, response and recovery."

More than 2,600 people are employed full-time by FEMA. They work at the agency's headquarters in Washington, D.C., at regional offices all over the United States, and at FEMA's training center in Maryland. Another 4,000 people work for FEMA as standby disaster assistance personnel. These employees spring into action whenever disasters occur. FEMA also works with other organizations that are trained to deal with disasters and emergencies, including state and local emergency management agencies such as police and fire departments, other federal agencies, and associations such as the American Red Cross.

Americans can count on the Federal Emergency Management Agency to step in and help.

The History of FEMA

The first time the U.S. government stepped in to deal with disaster was nearly 200 years ago. After a big fire devastated a New Hampshire town, the government passed the Congressional Act of 1803, which organized disaster aid to the town. Over the next 150 years, more than 100 separate acts would be passed to cope with various disasters ranging from fires and floods to hurricanes and earthquakes. However, creating hundreds of separate acts to deal with so many different kinds of disasters ended up being very complicated.

In the 1960s and early 1970s, a number of extremely destructive hurricanes and earthquakes devastated parts of the United States. And when hazards associated with nuclear power plants and the spilling and leakage of dangerous materials began to occur in the '70s, it became even more problematic for the federal government to deal with disaster. By this time, there were over 100 different federal organizations involved in various aspects of disaster relief. There were also hundreds of local and state organizations. The problem was that all of them worked separately.

It became clear that there needed to be more cooperation between America's many emergency and disaster relief agencies.

It was also decided that disaster relief efforts would be more efficient if they were all coordinated by one person—the president. Because of this, in 1979, President Jimmy Carter merged many of the separate disaster agencies into one big agency: the new Federal Emergency Management Agency.

FEMA's first director was John Macy. Under Macy, FEMA created an integrated emergency management system that could deal with any kind of disaster, large or small, natural or man-made, from a small fire to the ultimate disaster: full-scale war. And in its early years, the new agency had many unusual disasters to deal with. Catastrophes ranged from the 1979 accident at Three Mile Island, a nuclear power station in Pennsylvania that began releasing dangerous radioactive gases, to the 1980 Cuban refugee crisis, in which boatloads of poor refugees fleeing Cuba on rafts tried to reach the coast of Florida.

In 2001, Joe M. Allbaugh was appointed FEMA's new director by President George W. Bush. Months later, the terrorist attacks of September 11 shifted FEMA's focus to issues of national preparedness and domestic security. FEMA's Office of National Preparedness now works to make sure that emergency teams are equipped to deal with weapons of mass destruction such as nuclear bombs and biological weapons such as anthrax. To meet these new challenges and help communities face the threat of terrorism, FEMA has received billions of dollars in funding from the government.

FEMA-coordinated urban search and rescue workers help to search for victims in the rubble caused by powerful earthquakes in Mexico in 1985. FEMA frequently offers assistance to disaster emergency efforts outside the United States.

Urban Search and Rescue

In the early 1980s, the Fairfax County Fire and Rescue Department in Virginia and the Miami-Dade County Fire Department in Florida created special urban search and rescue (US&R) teams. These teams were highly trained to carry out rescue operations in collapsed buildings. Working with the U.S. State Department and the Office of Foreign Disaster Assistance (OFDA), these teams were invited by foreign governments to give much-needed support when serious disasters such as earthquakes and hurricanes overwhelmed the efforts of foreign search and rescue workers. When disastrous earthquakes struck Mexico City in 1985, Armenia in 1988, and the Philippines in 1990, these US&R teams immediately boarded American military aircraft and hours later were on-site ready to help out.

These teams were so effective that in 1991, FEMA decided to create its own special US&R teams as part of its Federal Response Plan. The results are the twenty-eight national US&R task forces that are staffed and equipped to carry out search-and-rescue operations in the wake of natural and man-made disasters. As their name indicates, US&R teams specialize in large-scale collapses of concrete buildings, generally in cities. However, their expertise might also be used in all sorts of emergencies, ranging from tornadoes and typhoons to spills of dangerous substances, technological accidents, and terrorist activities.

What differentiates FEMA US&R teams from the average rescue teams is that each US&R task force is made up of a complete mobile rescue unit—that is, a fully equipped rescue team that can respond to a disaster anywhere at a moment's notice. These teams consist of trained rescue workers as well as doctors, search specialists, communications experts, dog handlers, and many other specialists. And unlike smaller, local teams with less funding, personnel, and training, US&R teams can deal with long-term, large-scale rescue operations that last for days or even weeks.

When a disaster occurs, US&R teams are involved in finding and rescuing victims. They work twenty-four hours a day. Because of their highly specialized skills, when disaster strikes US&R teams are the first to respond. In the "front lines" of dangerous operations, these courageous men and women are willing to risk their lives to save ours.

CHAPTER 2

A Team of Specialists

There are currently twenty-eight FEMA US&R task forces based in various states across the United States. Eight task forces are in California, and both Florida and Virginia have two. The states of Arizona, Colorado, Indiana, Maryland, Massachusetts, Missouri, Nebraska, Nevada, New Mexico, New York, Ohio, Pennsylvania, Tennessee, Texas, Utah, and Washington each have one task force.

All of these task forces can be deployed at any time, at any disaster site within the United States. Two teams, however—Florida's Miami-Dade Task Force and Virginia's Fairfax County Task Force—also work together on the United States International Rescue Team. As part of the Office of Foreign Disaster Assistance, they have been sent to many disasters around the world at the invitation of foreign governments.

Members of FEMA's search and rescue unit survey the wreckage of the Albert P. Murrah Federal Building in Oklahoma City, Oklahoma, on April 20, 1995, one day after American terrorist Timothy McVeigh blew up the building with a truck bomb.

See How They Work

If a disaster is very serious, FEMA will decide that it's necessary for national US&R task forces to help local and state rescue and emergency workers. Within six hours, the three task forces that are closest to the disaster will be on-site to help locate and rescue victims. If further help is needed, more US&R task forces may be sent.

There are usually between 130 and 200 people on a US&R task force. Only 62, however, are actually sent to a disaster site. The others are summoned if a second task force is needed. For instance, if a disaster is major and the rescue operation goes on for a long time, the second task force will be sent to relieve the first one.

A single task force consists of two teams, each with thirty-one people, four search dogs, and a complete set of tools and equipment. The members of each team are divided into four areas of specialization: search experts, rescue experts, technical experts, and medical experts.

Search Experts

Search experts work to find trapped victims who are still alive. To do so, they use highly sensitive electronic tools such as high-tech Search Cams, fiber-optic cameras, and listening devices. They also use specially trained search dogs. Many search experts are trained electronics specialists. Others are dog handlers who have years of experience working with trained rescue dogs.

Team Players

Each FEMA task force has the following positions:

Search Experts:
2 search managers
2 search specialists
4 canine specialists

Rescue Experts:
2 rescue team managers
4 rescue squad officers
20 rescue specialists

Technical Experts:
2 technical team managers
2 technical information specialists
2 communications specialists
2 hazardous material (hazmat) specialists
2 heavy rigging specialists
4 logistics specialists
2 structures specialists

Medical Experts:
2 medical team managers
2 medical specialists

Rescue Experts

Rescue experts are the core members of the task force. Their main job is to free victims by safely digging them out from beneath tons of collapsed rubble. Using special techniques and equipment, they are able to remove victims from tight, difficult-to-reach spaces. Of course, before rescuing victims, rescue workers must make sure that the disaster site is as safe as possible. As such, some rescue workers are structural engineers whose job it is to explore the site, evaluate danger zones, and try to make dangerous collapsed structures as stable as possible for rescue operations.

In general, a rescue team is made up of four rescue squads with two rescue team managers. Each rescue squad consists of one rescue squad officer and five rescue specialists. Most often the rescue team is divided into two twelve-hour shifts. One shift works during the day, the other during the night. However, in the early stages of a really big disaster, everybody works together in order to increase the chances of finding living victims.

Technical Experts

Technical experts are specialists who know all about the metal and concrete structures of buildings. They study all parts of the disaster site, indicating dangerous spots and advising how to stabilize unsafe structures. In a nutshell, their job is to make sure rescuers themselves stay safe.

Technical experts have a wide range of expertise. Hazardous materials (or hazmat) specialists know all about the potential dangers of various materials such as gases or toxic substances that might escape following an accident. Structures specialists are engineers who can assess structures and give precise advice on how to safely move, stabilize, or remove different kinds of debris. They are constantly on guard for any shifting or movement in or around the disaster site.

Heavy equipment and rigging specialists know all about operating cranes, bulldozers, and other heavy equipment that

Jerry Jarrell, former director of the National Hurricane Center, reviews the hurricane update on the FEMA Web site. The center watches for hurricane developments over the Atlantic, Caribbean, Gulf of Mexico and eastern Pacific during hurricane season (May 15 through November 30).

is needed for clearing debris from a disaster site. Rigging refers to the network of structures put into place to prop up, secure, and stabilize the rubble of a building. Rubble is generally propped up—or "shored up"—by making special frames out of lumber that is carefully placed together.

Communications specialists are in charge of keeping open all communications systems—portable and shortwave radios, cell phones, and satellite transmitters—between different members of the task force. The technical information specialist's job is to document the entire rescue mission. He or she writes reports and uses cameras to record the operation in photos and on video. Finally, logistics specialists are responsible for keeping the task force's equipment all together and in working order.

Medical Experts

Medical experts provide medical attention to trapped and rescued victims as well as rescuers (including search dogs) who might suffer accidents on-site. They include physicians, nurses, and paramedics (assistants trained to deal with medical emergencies and the transportation of emergency victims). The minute they arrive on the scene, they get to work setting up a mobile hospital as close to the site as possible.

US&R medical experts are specially trained to deal with hazardous materials, to manage stress, and to treat people in confined, narrow spaces as well as people who have been crushed. Some also have veterinary experience which allows them to care for sick or injured search dogs.

Getting Onto a US&R Task Force

Getting onto a US&R task force is a challenging process. First of all, you need to have a great deal of specialized training in various aspects of search and rescue techniques. Even then, the waiting list to get on a task force is extremely long.

In most cases, the majority of team members come from one or several agencies. In the case of Virginia's Fairfax County Task Force, for example, aside from doctors that are trained in emergency procedures, structural engineers, communications experts, dog handlers, and heavy equipment and rigging specialists, all teams are made up of firefighters and paramedics from Fairfax County Fire and Rescue Department. As such, applying to get onto the task force is extremely difficult. It often takes years to get on a team.

Other task forces are made up of members from various agencies. Because of this, chances of getting on one of these task forces are higher. Massachusetts's task force, for example, not only has members from local fire departments, but also from local police forces and emergency management groups, and civilian volunteers from local volunteer search and rescue teams.

Getting onto a team as a civilian volunteer is easier than trying to get hired as an employee by a fire department. If you are interested in becoming a volunteer for a local S&R team, there are several groups that offer training programs. The national group that oversees all such rescue and recovery programs is the National Association for Search and Rescue (NASAR). Contacting them (at www.nasar.org) will give you information about local S&R groups near you, as well as training manuals and courses.

Training

The kind of training you need depends upon the position or specialty that you are interested in. One sure thing is that US&R is not for the faint of heart. Aside from physical strength and endurance, you need to have courage, determination, people skills, and the ability to deal with high stress as well as terrifying, dangerous, and often tragic situations. You will be around people who are suffering, dying, or dead. And frequently, you will be placing yourself at great personal risk.

Assuming that you meet all these requirements, training often includes thousands of hours of course work and practice drills over a period of at least several years. Obviously, medical specialists need to be licensed physicians, paramedics, or nurses, and structural engineers need to have university engineering degrees. Beyond these professional requirements, all task force members need to undergo training that will allow them to deal with emergency and disaster situations. For example, aside from having a minimum of five years' rescue experience, rescue team managers, rescue squad officers, and rescue specialists need to take courses such as Rope Rescue, Confined Space Rescue, Trench Rescue, Structural Collapse Rescue (both Heavy and Light/Medium), and Swift Water Rescue.

Even once you're part of a task force, you have to train regularly to maintain your skills and stay up-to-date with the latest equipment and rescue techniques. For example, members of Maryland's Montgomery County's search and rescue team—known as Maryland Task Force 1—train at least once a month in their specialty. They also cross-train and learn about other areas of US&R.

For their training, the Maryland Task Force built an area called the Rescue Mall. This "mall" includes a large classroom and a conference room. Specially built props allow trainees to carry out operations in structures that simulate collapsed buildings and small tunnel-like spaces. There are also concrete breaching stations where trainees can practice breaching and shoring-up techniques used to stabilize unsteady rubble. The Rescue Mall also features "Da Spider," a labyrinth of tubes that can be arranged to imitate different types of confined spaces.

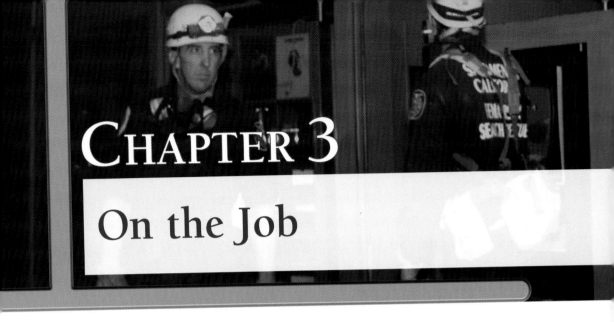

CHAPTER 3

On the Job

Every search and rescue operation is different. However, many procedures and tasks are common to all US&R efforts. The following is a portrait of a typical rescue operation.

Portrait of a Rescue

When a disaster hits, the first response is local. Fire departments, emergency teams, and local and state police forces closest to the disaster site are the first to arrive and begin rescue operations. If the disaster is serious, the local emergency manager might ask the state for help. And if it is really large-scale, the state may in turn ask for federal aid, in which case FEMA will decide to send the three closest task forces to help out.

As soon as they get to the site, the FEMA team meets with the local firefighter or emergency specialist who is in charge of rescue operations. After updates and briefings, some team members set up an operations base that includes tents and all

A New York City police officer escorts a traumatized office worker from the twin towers in New York City after the first World Trade Center bombing on February 26, 1993.

equipment. Meanwhile, search and rescue experts and structures specialists scout out the site, looking for likely search areas and potential dangers such as rubble that could collapse or hazardous gases or chemicals that might leak. Logistics specialists get in touch with local suppliers in order to get heavy equipment, lumber for shoring, food, portable toilets, and other supplies.

Once the team has its base set up, in order to get an idea of the extent of the damage, searchers and rescuers begin to carefully explore areas that are less likely to collapse. After examining blueprints of the building to understand its structure, they mark areas that need bracing (support) and areas where victims have been spotted. If any live victims are found during this first sweep, the search stops immediately. Structures are stabilized so that victims can be rescued. Once this preliminary search is finished, a detailed search begins with cameras, listening devices, and dogs. Medics give aid to any victims who are found alive.

Once the safest areas have been searched, more dangerous regions of the site will have to be shored up and made more stable before further searches can continue. In a sense, what teams have to do is "de-layer" the site. When a building collapses, layers of rubble fall on top of each other like a house of cards. Between the layers are narrow spaces where victims may be trapped. The trick is to dig from top to bottom and from the outside to the inside. Otherwise, the pile could collapse again, threatening rescuers and killing those who are trapped.

As more areas are shored up, searchers can go deeper into the rubble, exploring caves and tunnels invisible from the surface. Searching continues as long as there's a chance of finding live victims.

When a victim is found, the search group begins the dangerous and delicate task of breaking and cutting through thousands of pounds of crushed and twisted concrete, metal, glass, and wood to get to the victim. To remove debris from the fragile center of the site, rescuers resort to "bucket brigades." A human chain is formed, with rescuers passing buckets filled with rubble from person to person, and then to large trucks that can haul it away. This task takes a long time and is physically draining, but bringing heavy equipment such as bulldozers and cranes to the center of the site would destabilize the already unstable structure, risking the lives of both rescuers and victims. Heavy equipment is moved in once it has been decided that there is no possible chance of survivors.

The greatest risk to rescuers is being crushed by the sudden collapse of an unstable structure. Meanwhile, cuts, scrapes, broken bones, burns, and respiratory infections due to the inhalation of hazardous fumes and gases, dust, and carbon monoxide are all common. Rescuers also have increased chances of acquiring diseases such as diphtheria, tetanus, and pneumonia.

While the rescue operations are being carried out, hazmat experts check for any dangerous materials that might have leaked or escaped. They also decontaminate team members who may have come into contact with toxic chemicals or decomposing bodies. Once there is no chance of finding live victims, US&R teams' missions are finished and they return home.

Armenian Earthquake—FEMA to the Rescue

In 1988, a massive earthquake hit Armenia, part of the former Soviet Union (Russia). The following excerpts are from the first-hand account of Batallion Chief Michael Tamillow, a member of FEMA's Virginia's Fairfax County Task Force, who participated in the rescue operations. His full account can be found at the task force Web site (http://www.vatf1.org/).

At 11:30 PM on Friday, December 10, 1988, Tamillow received a phone call at home that nearly knocked him "off [his] feet." There had been a catastrophic earthquake in Armenia. The international section of Tamillow's Technical Rescue Operations Team was to prepare itself immediately to fly to the earthquake site. They had less than twelve hours before take-off time!

Upon their arrival, the team found the Soviet airport in a state of chaos. Aircraft from many countries were busy unloading equipment and supplies. An army-sized group of Armenian citizens and Soviet military personnel immediately began to unload the FEMA team's C-141 military plane by hand. It took them over four hours to move more than 30 tons (30.5 tonnes) of supplies onto eight trucks and a bus that would carry the American team to the devastated city of Leninakan.

Aftermath

Even though FEMA task force members have years of experience, the sight of dead, maimed, and injured victims, griefstricken survivors, and devastated areas of a city can be very traumatizing. Even once a mission is over, rescue workers may have difficulty dealing with disturbing moments and memories.

To help teams deal with the psychological effects of what they experience, or emotions associated with unsuccessful rescue attempts, FEMA usually organizes a debriefing session. After a mission, debriefers return with team members and spend time with them to see how everybody is coping. Back at home, team members meet with crisis and mental health counselors. Counselors keep in touch with troubled team members and also give support to members' friends and family.

Tamillow recalls the trip: "[We] finally boarded an old city bus (which had no heat) for a hair-raising ride over icy roads and a high mountain pass to our area of operation." Under usual circumstances the trip would have taken two and a half hours. This time however, it took more than five. Delays were

FEMA task force members and local emergency crews remove a body from a site that was destroyed by the devastating earthquake in Armenia in 1998.

caused by a combination of bad weather and the horrible traffic jams created by the many relief vehicles trying to enter the city while citizens in their own cars attempted to get those who had survived the earthquake out of the city.

As Tamillow recalls, there were quite a few times when the bus would suddenly slide sideways because the road was covered with so much ice. "The shoulders dropped off 10 to 20 feet (3 to 6 meters) on both sides of the road. I could only ponder our fate should the bus plunge off the edge," he says.

Upon their arrival, the American rescue team was thrown into a situation far worse than any they had ever imagined. Leninakan, a city of 225,000 inhabitants had been completely destroyed.

Tamillow divided his team into two groups. One group occupied the camp that was set up on the edge of town. They were in charge of guarding equipment, finding supplies and making food. The other group of searchers with dogs was sent out into the midst of the devastated city in the hopes of finding survivors.

That first afternoon, Tamillow, who was at the camp, received a radio transmission from the rescue group. Although it was six days after the earthquake had struck, the rescue team had found a survivor. It took five hours to rescue a sixty-year-old woman who had been pinned under heavy rubble and concrete. "It was quite frustrating for us back at camp not to be able to assist them," confesses Tamillow. "We had no transportation available."

Lack of sleep, cold weather, and sheer physical effort took its toll on the rescue workers. The woman was trapped by the dead bodies of a baby and a young girl. Recalls Tamillow: "One of the emergency physicians on our team had to amputate the leg of the girl to allow for her removal prior to the extrication of the live woman. It was grim work." Finally, when night had already fallen, the woman was freed and taken to a hospital.

"The remaining days spent in Leninakan were a series of frustrating trips in and around the city chasing rumors and assessing hopeless sites," remembers Tamillow. "It was an ordeal that required a great deal of effort just to survive."

Both water and firewood were extremely hard to come by. Back at the camp, Tamillow and his team scrounged around for anything they could find. Meanwhile, the severe cold made even the smallest activity that much more difficult. "In the cold climate we would have given anything for a decent bathroom. As it was, we had to construct a makeshift latrine [toilet] out in an adjacent field…[For food] we were usually too tired to do more than open a can of chili or spaghetti and eat it out of the can."

It was also difficult to obtain the gasoline that was necessary to operate power tools. In the end, the team had to barter, or trade, to get a few gallons of gas wherever they could.

Later on, several very vivid scenes left permanent impressions in Tamillow's memory:

"I'll never forget standing outside a collapsed three-story building talking to a local interpreter. This building had been a grade school. What was left looked like the open side of a child's dollhouse, with a few rooms left intact including the desks and blackboards. The vast majority of the school children died in the rubble as three-quarters of the building collapsed. The earthquake occurred at 11:41 AM on Wednesday morning. The interpreter began crying as she relayed the fact that, had the earthquake occurred five minutes later, most all of the children probably would have survived. All schools let their students outside for recess at 11:45 AM each day. This seemed a cruel twist of fate…"

In the end, Tamillow believes the FEMA team left a significant impact on many of the city's survivors. Throughout their stay, they were approached by hundreds of people who couldn't thank them enough for all they had done. Tamillow says that, "I think our concern diminished somewhat their immense pain and suffering."

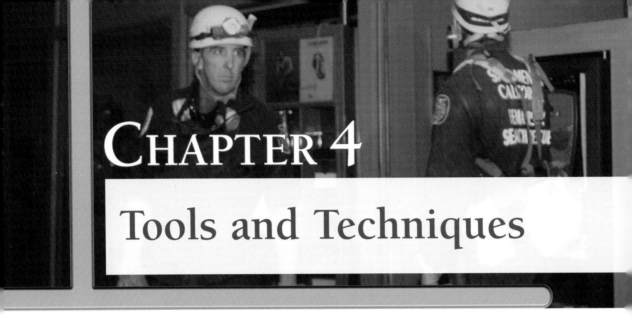

CHAPTER 4

Tools and Techniques

Every FEMA task force has an emergency equipment kit that includes absolutely everything a team will need during a rescue operation. Usually emergency kits contain around 16,400 separate tools and pieces of equipment, weigh around 60,000 pounds (4,003 kilograms), and are worth about $1.4 million.

Logistics specialists are responsible for all of this equipment. They must make sure that they have everything necessary to set up an area that is a combination of mobile emergency hospital, construction site, communications center, high-tech engineering firm, and camp with sleeping and eating facilities. Aside from making rescue operations quick and efficient, it avoids placing a burden on local suppliers at the disaster site who likely have no equipment to spare. For this last reason in particular, task forces must have everything to keep them totally self-sufficient for at least their first four days.

All of this equipment can be grouped into five categories:

Search and rescue equipment: Similar to the equipment at any construction site. Ordinary building materials such as drills, jackhammers, saws for cutting concrete, and lumber (for shoring and breaching) are required. Lumber—along with rope—is also used to safely remove victims from the rubble.

Technical equipment: Very high-tech. There are more than 500 pieces of equipment. Tiny snake-shaped, highly sensitive cameras and fiber-optic scopes—known as Search Cams

A FEMA communications specialist sets up a satellite dish linking FEMA to one of its mobile disaster recovery centers. These centers help to speed up the process of delivering aid to disaster victims.

and Snake Eyes—can register the slightest of human motions. This proves extremely useful when dealing with victims who are caught beneath rubble where neither dogs nor humans can go. They can light up dark areas and are small enough to be lowered through a crack in the floor. Super-sensitive listening devices can detect even the slightest human sound and locate victims who are still alive.

Searching for survivors after a disaster is a race against time. Experience has shown that victims who are trapped in a collapsed building can often hear rescue workers, but cannot make themselves be heard through the layers of concrete that have trapped them. However, if victims are able to knock, scratch, or move, the collapsed structure often carries these sounds. Although they can't be heard by a human ear, they can be detected by sensitive listening devices such as the Delsar Life Detector.

The Delsar uses special sensors that can pick up extremely tiny vibrations sent through solid matter or gases and convert them into signals that can be seen or heard by rescue workers. The Life Detectors' lightweight and wide-ranging sensors, as well as the fact that rescue workers can plant and listen to many sensors at the same time, means that search teams can cover large areas. Often, rescue workers use magnets to attach sensors to beams, which magnify sound. They also use elimination filters that block out surrounding sounds such as people talking and machines rumbling.

Medical equipment: Every kind of medical supply that one could require in an emergency situation. Aside from all sorts of medicines, common supplies include blankets, intravenous liquids, bone saws, scalpels, burn treatments, suture sets (for stitching wounds), airways, tracheal tubes (tubes that allow victims to keep breathing), and defibrillators (electronic devices that give an electric shock to a heart that has stopped beating).

Communications equipment: Allows rescuers to stay in touch with each other and with task force leaders. Communication is especially crucial in the event that a victim is found, an accident occurs, or a collapse requires rescue workers to evacuate the scene. Cell phones, laptop computers, radios, generators, and lights are some of the most commonly used types of equipment.

Often, rescue workers communicate by leaving messages for each other written on the walls of a collapsed building. FEMA task forces at work at Ground Zero in New York City left the following messages for each other after searching specific areas:

VA-TF1 The name of the task force that searched the area (Virginia Task Force-1)

13/09/01 1100 The date (September 13, 2001) and time (11 AM) the area was searched

2 LIVE The number of survivors found

Food to the Rescue

After twelve hours of sifting through rubble, saving victims with horrible injuries, and recovering dead bodies, rescue workers are exhausted. They are also hungry. Luckily, there are MREs.

MRE stands for "meals ready to eat." These are meals in pouches that are easy for rescue workers to prepare. These meals are a lot more sophisticated than your average cheese sandwich or "just add water" soup. One MRE, for example, includes a main course, a side dish, a dessert, crackers, and a beverage base. All this for about $2. Meals are sealed in airless pouches that can be dropped by parachute, with a 100-percent survival rate. The pouches can withstand heavy-duty shaking and vibrations and lots of pressure.

Although all meals can be eaten at room temperature, some are self-heating (with special heating pouches). Others can be warmed up simply by placing them close to a heat source: a radiator, an engine, even your own body. The meals themselves remain edible for up to ten years. And what meals they are: ham and shrimp jambalaya, beef enchilada in gravy, smoked salmon fillet, and for dessert, the likes of pineapple poundcake.

6 DEAD The number of dead victims found

RATS Dangers to be aware of

Logistics equipment: All the basic survival supplies that task force members will need as they work in twelve-hour shifts around the clock. Food, water, cots, sleeping bags, rain gear, and cold-weather gear are some examples. The following is the Pennsylvania Task Force's personal equipment list published on their Web site:

Standard Pennsylvania Task Force uniform, consisting of:
> 2 navy-blue battle dress uniform tops
> 3 navy-blue battle dress uniform pants
> 4 gray T-shirts with Pennsylvania-Task Force 1

Personal protective gear, consisting of:
> 1 helmet with chin strap
> 1 pair safety glasses with side protection or safety goggles
> 2 sets of hearing protection
> 1 pair leather work gloves
> 1 pair protective boots with steel toe
> 2 quarts of water in canteens with belt

Additional items:
> 6 pair underwear
> 6 pair cotton socks

2 pair shorts

1 pair thongs or sandals

2 sets of "meals ready to eat" or equivalent

1 collapsible cup

1 pair sunglasses

1 pair non-work shoes

1 physical training clothing

1 pen and notepad

1 toiletry kit, with soap, toothpaste, razor with extra blades, deodorant, toilet paper

1 Chap Stick

1 sunscreen

1 bug spray

1 alarm clock

1 personal first-aid kit

1 week's supply of personal prescription medications

1 sleeping bag

1 pillow

2 sheets

3 bandannas

1 uniform jumpsuit

1 rain gear

1 baseball cap

1 helmet with light with extra bulb and batteries

1 flashlight with extra bulb and batteries

1 credit card

cash

1 Field Operations Guide manual

1 wallet

1 camera with film

1 jackknife

1 sweatshirt/fleece jacket

1 sock liner

1 Coolmax underwear

1 pair spare boots, Gortex lined

1 pair Gortex socks

1 wide brim hat

mosquito netting

1 bug headnet

Robots to the Rescue

After the attacks on the World Trade Center, over a dozen whirring machines arrived at Ground Zero and went plowing through the rubble alongside human and canine rescuers. Short, squat, and ugly, they looked a lot more like tiny military tanks than C-3PO and R2-D2 from *Star Wars*. Nevertheless, robots could be the big rescue heroes of future disasters.

Unlike humans, robots don't suffer from stress, exhaustion, or horror. And unlike dogs, robots don't have their keen sense of smell obstructed by smoke and dust. It was the first time ever that robots had been used in a US&R operation. And the results were very promising.

The remote-controlled machines ranged in size from a shoebox to a suitcase and cost between $15,000 and $30,000 each. They can flatten themselves to squeeze through tight spaces and "stand" in order to "see" over chunks of rubble. Many are small enough to go down narrow sewage pipes. Outfitted with lights, sensors, video cameras, and Caterpillar-like treads, they crawl around and underneath smashed concrete and twisted steel, searching for victims in places where dogs and humans cannot and dare not go. Some robots, such as the Talon, have arms and lobster-like pincers. Others, such as the Packbot, have flippers that allow it to climb hills and stairs. And the Urbot can even function upside down.

With remote controls that resemble computer game joysticks, robots can be lowered to depths of up to 30 feet (9.14 meters). Their cameras send images up to rescue workers, while microphones capture voices and human sounds. Some robots have heat-sensitive thermal cameras that can detect body heat. Others are programmed to search for colors amidst the gray dust that covers everything. A tiny dot of red, whether fabric or blood, can be easily identified and used to alert a rescue team.

Following September 11, robots were successful in finding many bodies and were used for surveying several damaged buildings around the disaster site. The only problem—aside from the extreme heat that melted the robots' rubber treads—was that there were so few of them.

Experts predict that if hundreds of robots had been quickly put into action, rescue efforts would have been much easier and more efficient. Retired Lieutenant Colonel John Blitch, a U.S. Army robotics expert who coordinated the robot rescuers, told the *New York Times*: "Everyone that physically saw them was impressed by the technology. The Fire Department loved them."

Only days before the World Trade Center attacks, Colonel Blitch had "retired" the robots that were part of a program for robotic search and rescue. On September 11, they were in the basement of his house in Washington, D.C. When Blitch heard the news of the attacks, he packed the robots into his car and drove all the way to the disaster site in lower Manhattan.

The robots that helped out at Ground Zero are an example of how US&R operations will be conducted in years to come. In the future, sites that are too hot or dangerous for humans and dogs will be sifted through immediately by robots. Similarly, robots will be able to explore sites contaminated by hazardous chemicals and toxic biological substances. In a few years, technology will be more sophisticated and robots more independent. They will be faster, cheaper, and capable of saving more lives.

CHAPTER 5

Canines to the Rescue

Dogs have long been used in rescue missions. Because they are naturally endowed with very strong senses of hearing and smell that far surpass those of humans, they are ideal for tracking down buried victims who can't be seen by human rescue workers. That dogs are obedient, faithful, hardworking, and affectionate also makes them ideal partners in rescue missions. In fact, many dogs often serve as unofficial mascots for FEMA US&R teams.

Years of Training

In order to serve on a FEMA task force, dogs, along with their human handlers, must pass a tough US&R national certification program. Though it may be hard to believe, getting certified is a lot more difficult for dogs than for their handlers. The non-profit, volunteer-operated National Disaster Search Dog Foundation (NDSDF) is an organization responsible for training and certifying FEMA dog/handler rescue teams. The NDSDF finds search dogs, trains them, and matches them with handlers.

Search dogs have to prove they have the following skills in order to become certified:

- Barking skills to alert human rescuers when a victim is found

- Agility skills to be able to navigate through rubble

- Obedience and comprehension skills to be able to listen carefully to handlers' commands and obey handlers' orders in the midst of chaotic situations

A FEMA search and rescue dog searches through the rubble of a store in San Juan, Puerto Rico, on November 1996, following an explosion that was caused by a gas leak.

- Courage and determination to overcome their natural fear of tunnels, closed spaces, and shaky or unstable surfaces

There are two levels of certification for search dog/handler teams. To receive basic certification, dogs must be able to perform specific search and rescue tasks under the supervision and guidance of their handlers. To receive advanced certification, dogs must perform these same tasks and more difficult ones— on their own.

Training for advanced certification includes going through a tricky rescue simulation course during which dogs are distracted from their mission by false scents, food, and smoke that gets in their eyes and goes up their noses. For most dogs, it takes thousands of hours and several years of training just to achieve basic certification. Very few dogs ever receive advanced certification. Those who do are truly a breed apart.

According to the NDSDF, there is currently a great need for several hundred new dog/handler teams that can be deployed in the event of a national disaster. The NDSDF estimates that it costs between $10,000 and $15,000 to fully train just one dog/handler team to FEMA certification standards. Furthermore, in order to take part in FEMA US&R operations, teams need to be recertified every two years.

The Ideal Candidate

Of course, not just any friendly mutt can become a search dog. In general, sporting dogs are used. Experience has shown that the best search dogs tend to be German shepherds, Labrador retrievers, golden retrievers, and retriever mixes. While most dogs are natural hunters, these dogs tend to have the sharpest hunting instincts. However, any healthy dog that is very playful (good at playing hide-and-seek, for example) and shows strong retriever tendencies, can be considered for a search-dog training program if he or she passes certain tests.

Very few search dogs are donated by owners. Instead, the NDSDF has groups that visit animal shelters in search of promising candidates. Dogs get started young, usually between the ages of two months and ten months. This is not only because training takes such a long time, but because young pups learn more quickly and don't have time to form bad habits.

The Human Element

No dog works alone. The success of a search dog depends on the close partnership between the dog and his or her human handler. Like dogs, humans must go through years of training with their canine partners before becoming certified for a team. Certification requires handlers to pass oral and written exams dealing with search and rescue techniques. They must also have highly developed dog-handling skills.

Most handlers are firefighters. This is because most search and rescue workers on FEMA task forces are firefighters who have gone through special US&R training. Many fire stations have their own trained dogs that help out during local disasters and search and rescue operations. Volunteers who want to join FEMA task forces and have gone through all the necessary US&R training can sometimes be dog handlers, too. Aside from being in top physical shape and loving dogs a great deal,

FEMA worker Erick Robertson pets Pork Chop, a one-year-old search and rescue dog who is being treated for dehydration. Many emergency workers receive instruction in dog-handling as part of their training.

volunteers must meet with firefighters for search and rescue training with dogs, usually at least twice a week. It's important to bond with your dog and to make sure that he or she remains well-disciplined and in top shape.

Dogs who work with firefighters generally live with firefighters and their families. They are raised and treated as pets while they go through training. Once a dog/handler team receives FEMA US&R certification, dogs go to work and come home each day with their firefighter handlers. Sharing their lives in such a way, it's not surprising that many dogs and handlers develop extremely close relationships.

Of course, search dogs get time off, too. When not at work or training, dogs relax with handlers and their families. But even at the fire station, dogs have special beds where they can rest and a whole slew of toys with which to play.

On the Job

When a disaster strikes, dogs travel to the site—along with the rest of their team and all emergency equipment—by bus, truck, boat, helicopter, or military aircraft. On site, they immediately get to work, sniffing through the rubble for signs of life. They walk over chunks of debris and crawl through dark tunnels. They are even trained to climb ladders. Whenever they find the scent of a possible survivor, they bark.

"Sniffer" dogs are actually trained to bark nonstop for thirty seconds if they think they've located a victim. A second dog is then brought in. If the second dog barks for thirty seconds too, search equipment is used as a final confirmation before beginning a rescue operation.

Top Dog

Rob Cima has been a fire chief with the El Dorado County Fire District in California for over twenty years. He is also a rescue technician and canine search specialist for California's Sacramento County FEMA Task Force—along with his trusted partner Harley, a seven-year-old golden retriever.

Rob and Harley first met at the local Humane Society. Harley had ended up there because the family who owned him thought he was hyperactive, destructive, and out-of-control. He was scheduled to be put to sleep when Rob found him. Rob entered Harley in the NDSDF training program. During training, Harley was neither hyperactive nor destructive nor out-of-control. In fact, he received his basic certification in 1998 (at the age of three) and today (at the age of seven) he is a certified advanced search dog.

Search dogs are constantly alert for signs from their two-legged partners. At the blast of a whistle from their handlers, they stop immediately, wherever they are, ready for new orders.

Obedience coupled with a natural sense of balance and agility keeps dogs safe on shifting surfaces. Even so, all dogs have booties that they can wear to protect their paws from hot or rough surfaces. However, in situations where lots of rain or mud makes getting around slippery, dogs often have better traction without the booties.

Like humans, dogs can sometimes find rescue work discouraging. In 1995, search dogs were used during the rescue operation that followed the bombing of Oklahoma City's Alfred P. Murrah Federal Building. FEMA task forces who arrived on the scene expected to save victims' lives. But the devastation was so great that, instead, they spent day after day recovering dead bodies.

Even the search dogs grew depressed by the lack of positive reinforcement that comes from finding live victims. "The dogs get a lot of praise when they find a live person. But in Oklahoma, we didn't go through the positive praise routine," said Wilma Melville, in "Oklahoma City: Healing the Heartache," published in *9-1-1 Magazine*. Melville is a canine specialist with FEMA's Los Angeles County Task Force 2 who searched with Murphy, her two-and-a-half-year-old black Labrador. To help boost their spirits, some members would hide in nearby damaged buildings so that the dogs could be sent in to find them. "When the dogs would alert, we would praise them. This helped keep them cheerful."

Heroes

The FEMA US&R task force members spent ten days in Oklahoma City. They worked night and day, until all hope of finding survivors had been exhausted. And even then, they still kept working. To a shocked and grieving city and nation, these rescuers were heroes. Donations of water, food, blankets, and other supplies poured in. So did the letters of thanks and appreciation.

The letters made Rescue Squad Officer Tod Mitcham, with FEMA's Los Angeles County Task Force, think about the meaning of heroism. "We do this kind of stuff, picking up twisted bodies, every day," he admitted in "Oklahoma City: Healing the Heartache." "But in Oklahoma, suddenly we were being called heroes, even though we were just doing our job."

Mitcham took time to answer the letters. "To me," he said, "a hero is not someone who is worshipped. A hero is not someone who has done something dramatic or dangerous. A hero is someone who thinks about others before thinking about himself."

Wilma Melville agreed. "Going to a disaster doesn't make you a hero," she pointed out. "The heroism is in the dedication to the work. Day after day, year after year, we train and work with the dogs, not knowing if we'll ever get called to an incident. The local people who called us heroes didn't seem to realize that it was our privilege to be there."

GLOSSARY

agile Physically quick and well-coordinated.

barter To bargain in order to trade one good or product for another.

brace To prop up, support.

breach To break through (a wall, for example) using a battering ram.

civilian A citizen who is not in the military or other service.

debriefing The session in which a specialist questions someone about a just-finished job or mission.

debris The remains of something that was destroyed.

deploy To send out on assignment.

differentiates Sets apart, distinguishes.

diphtheria A serious contagious disease that inflames the heart and nervous system.

extricate To remove, pull out.

girders The main horizontal structure of a bridge or building.

ground zero The center or point of origin of an intense or violent activity.

hazardous Dangerous.

jackhammer An air-operated tool used for drilling rocks.

latrine Toilet.

logistics The handling of the details of an operation or mission.

paramedics Medics trained to deal with medical emergencies and transportation of emergency victims.

rigging A network of structures used to prop up, secure, and stabilize parts of a collapsed building.

rubble The broken fragments of a building.

shore up To prop up using structures assembled from lumber.

tetanus A serious infectious disease that causes muscle spasms.

toxic Poisonous.

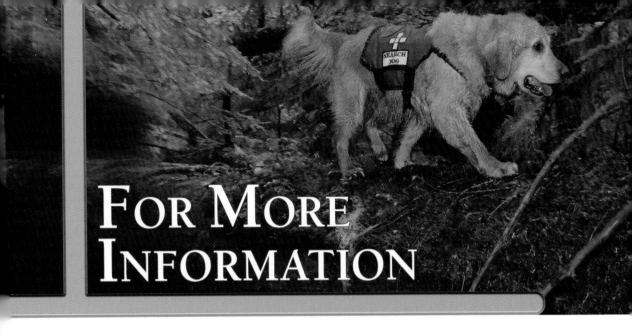

FOR MORE INFORMATION

American Rescue Dog Association
P.O. Box 151
Chester, NY 10918
Web site: http://www.ardainc.org

Federal Emergency Management Agency (FEMA)
Federal Center Plaza
500 C Street SW
Washington, DC 20472
(202) 566-1600
Web site: http://www.fema.gov

National Association of Search and Rescue (NASAR)
4500 Southgate Place, Suite 100
Chantilly, VA 20151-1714
(703) 222-6277
Web site: http://www.nasar.org

National Disaster Search Dog Foundation (NDSDF)
323 East Matilija Avenue, Suite 110-245
Ojai, CA 93023
(888) 646-1242
Web site: http://www.ndsdf.org

National Institute for Urban Search and Rescue (NIUSR)
P.O. Box 91648,
Santa Barbara, CA 93190
(805) 966-6178
Web site: http://www.niusr.org

Web Sites

Due to the changing nature of Internet links, the Rosen
Publishing Group, Inc., has developed an online list of Web
sites related to the subject of this book. This site is updated
regularly. Please use this link to access the list:

http://www.rosenlinks.com/csro/fema/

FOR FURTHER READING

Brin, Susannah. *Search and Rescue*. Irvine, CA: Saddleback Publishing, 1998.

George, Charles, and Linda George. *Search and Rescue Dogs*. Mankato, MN: Capstone Press, 1998.

Halley, Ned. *Disasters*. New York: Larousse Kingfisher Chambers, 1999.

Hampton, Wilborn. *Meltdown: A Race Against Nuclear Disaster at Three Mile Island*. Cambridge, MA: Candlewick Press, 2000.

Moore, Kevin, and Jack Challoner. *Eyewitness: Hurricane and Tornado*. New York: Dorling Kindersley, 2000.

Platt, Richard. *Disaster!: Catastrophes that Shook the World*. New York: Dorling Kindersley, 1997.

Wheeler, Jill C. *September 11, 2001: The Day that Changed America*, Vol. 1. Edina, MN: ABDO Publishing Company, 2002.

BIBLIOGRAPHY

The American Rescue Dog Association Web site. Retrieved April 2002 (http://www.ardainc.org/).

California US&R Task Force 3 Web site. Retrieved April 2002 (http://catf3.usar.org/).

Center for Robot Assisted Search and Rescue (CRASAR) Web site. Retrieved April 2002 (http://www.csee.usf.edu/robotics/crasar/).

FEMA Web site. Retrieved April 2002 (http://www.fema.gov).

Lee, Jennifer. "Agile in a Crisis, Robots Show Their Mettle." *The New York Times*, September 27, 2001.

Maryland Task Force 1 Web site. Retrieved April 2002 (http://www.co.mo.md.us/services/dfrs/mdtf1).

Massachusetts Task Force Web site. Retrieved April 2002 (http://www.matf.org/).

Miami-Dade Florida Task Force 1 Web site. Retrieved April 2002 (http://www.co.miami-dade.fl.us/firerescue/urban.htm).

National Association of Search and Rescue (NASAR) Web site. Retrieved April 2002 (http://www.nasar.org/).

National Disaster Search Dog Foundation (NDSDF) Web site. Retrieved April 2002 (http://www.ndsdf.org/).

National Institute for Urban Search and Rescue (NIUSR) Web site. Retrieved April 2002 (http://www.niusr.org/).

Pennsylvania Task Force 1 Web site. Retrieved April 2002 (http://www.pa-tf1.com/).

"Rescue and Recovery at World Trade Center, Pentagon." *The Seattle Times*. Retrieved April 2002 (http://seattletimes. nwsource.com/art/news/nation_world/terrorism/ rescue_15.pdf).

Rigg, Nancy J. "Oklahoma City: Healing the Heartache." *9-1-1 Magazine*. September/October 1995. Retrieved April 2002 (http://www.9-1-1magazine.com/magazine/OKCitySpecial/ 26healing/).

Sacramento Fire Department Urban Search and Rescue California Task Force 7 Web site. Retrieved April 2002 (http://www. smfd.ca.gov/USAR.HTM).

Tamillow, Michael. "Earthquake: Armenia, Russia," Virginia Fairfax County Urban Search and Rescue Team Web site. Retrieved April 2002 (http:vatfl.org/missionrussia.shtml).

Trivedi, Bijal P. "Search-and-Rescue Robots Tested at New York Disaster Site." *National Geographic Today*. September 14, 2001. Retrieved April 2002 (http://news.nationalgeographic. com/news/2001/09/0914_TVdisasterrobot.html).

Virginia Fairfax County Urban Search and Rescue Team Web site. Retrieved April 2002 (http://www.vatf1.org/).

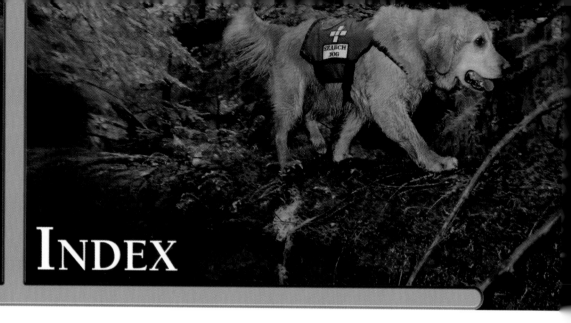

INDEX

About the Author

Greg A. Binney is a freelance writer who lives in Gallup, New Mexico.

Photo Credits

Cover © Vittoriano Rastelli/Corbis; p. 1 © AP/Wide World Photos; pp. 5, 6, 17 © Corbis; p. 9 © Dave Gatley/Corbis; p. 13 © Owen Franken/Corbis; p. 21 © Joe Cavaretta/AP/Wide World Photos; p. 27 © Mark Cardwell/Corbis; p. 32 © Peter Turnley/Corbis; p. 37 © TimePix; p. 47 © Jose Jimenez/AP/Wide World Photos; p. 50 © Suzanne Plunkett/AP/Wide World Photos.

Editor

Annie Sommers

Designer

Nelson Sá